WORKSTATION FLIP CHART

Phonics/ Word Study

D1299001

A

The **McGraw·Hill** Companies

Macmillan/McGraw-Hill

Published by Macmillan/McGraw-Hill, of McGraw-Hill Education, a division of The McGraw-Hill Companies, Inc., Two Penn Plaza, New York, New York 10121.

Printed in Colombia

1 2 3 4 5 6 7 8 9 QWB 14 13 12 11 10

Differentiate Instruction Using Workstation Flipchart Activities:

1. Assess to determine what students can do and what practice is needed. Use data to create mixed skill small groups. Model how to ask for and provide assistance in a group.

2. Assign a color name for each group: red, blue, yellow, green.

3. Use colored vinyl tabs on flipchart pages to indicate which group completes each activity. Change tabs to assign a specific activity per each group's needs.

4. Allow students to work collaboratively if the content or skill was recently introduced. Delay assigning activities as independent work until sufficient instruction and guided practice have occurred.

5. Encourage students to assist each other if you are unavailable or working with another group.

Teaching Tips:

- Ensure activity assignment can be completed within small group period or identify what students are to do with their work at the end of the instructional period, i.e., return to folder or notebook, complete as seatwork or homework.

- Have students read the flipchart page together in small group, and then discuss what they need to do. Consider assigning a group leader who monitors progress and provides assistance if needed.

- Suggestions for extending or modifying a particular activity may be printed on larger sticky notes and attached to a flipchart page or a clipboard. You may use color coded notes or clipboards (red, blue, yellow or green) to individualize instruction for each small group.

- Repeat some activities from the flipcharts for additional guided practice, review or assessment. Use the vinyl tabs to select the assignments for small group work that day and ask students to work independently at their desk to complete the activity.

Contents

- Using note cards or square pieces of paper, write a word on one card and its homophone on another. Make ten pairs.

- Shuffle the cards. Place them facedown. Take turns with a partner flipping two cards over at a time. When you flip over homophones, define each of the words. If you are correct, take the two cards. The person with the most cards wins.

Extension

- Repeat the game, using your partner's cards.

fair

fare

Things you need:
- note cards
- dictionary
- pen or pencil

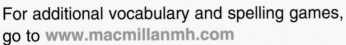

- Using a Layered Book Foldable, write one vowel at the bottom of each page. Each vowel should have its own page.

- On each page, write two words that have the short vowel sound of the vowel on the page. Add one word with a long vowel sound for each vowel and one word with a variant spelling for each short vowel sound.

- With a partner, practice pronouncing all your words correctly.

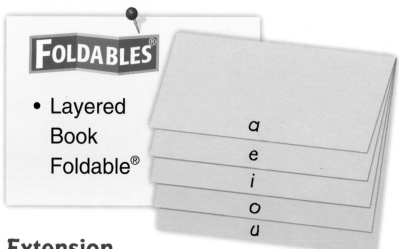

FOLDABLES

- Layered Book Foldable®

a
e
i
o
u

Extension

- With your partner, make sentences using as many of your words as possible in each sentence. Read the sentences aloud as fast as you can, being careful to pronounce all sounds correctly.

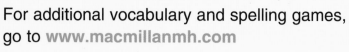

- Use a dictionary or online search engine to identify idioms and adages that feature the word *take,* such as "take charge" or "It takes a village to raise a child."

- Write sentences with "take" idioms and adages on strips of paper.

- Trade sentence strips with a partner.

- Take turns acting out scenes that demonstrate each idiom or adage.

Extension

- Adding other sentences to the sentence strips, write a scene from a play using as many "take" idioms and adages as you can.

- Perform the play for another pair of students.

Things you need:

- paper and pen or pencil
- scissors
- dictionary

- Using a dictionary create a list of words with long-vowel sounds on a nature theme. For example, words such as *rose, cave, leaf,* and *sky* all contain long vowel sounds.

- Use the list to create a landscape drawing containing all the items.

- Write a summary description of the landscape using the words.

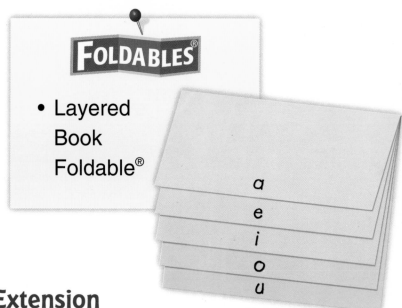

FOLDABLES®

- Layered Book Foldable®

a
e
i
o
u

Extension

Using a Layered Book Foldable®, sort your words by writing a different long vowel on each layer of the Foldable, and writing your words on the layers of the vowel sounds that they match.

- Write a paragraph describing a monument using words ending in *-ed* or *-ing.*

- Exchange papers with a partner. Underline all words with inflectional endings *-ed* and *-ing*.

Extension

- Combine your ideas and collaborate on a new paragraph.

- Discuss how the meaning changes if you change the inflectional endings.

Things you need:

- paper and pen or pencil

- dictionary

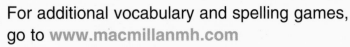

Words with /ü/, /ū/, /u̇/

- Label the pockets of a Three-pocket Foldable® with the following three vowel sounds: /ü/ ("oo") as in *loon*; /ū/ ("yoo") as in *mule*; and /u̇/ ("oo") as in *book*.

- Write four words for each sound on note cards. Working with a partner, read each of the cards aloud and have your partner place the cards in the pockets of the correct vowel sound. Play until every pocket is filled correctly. Then play again using your partner's card and Foldable.

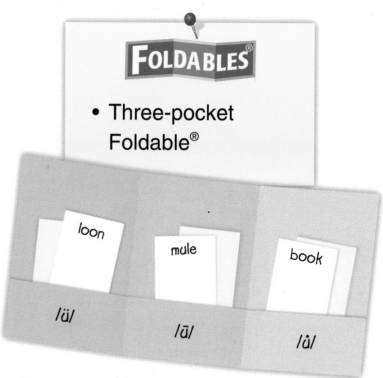

- Three-pocket Foldable®

Extension

- Combine the two decks of cards and play with another team.

- Using a Three-pocket Foldable®, mark one pocket with the suffix *-ous,* one with *-tion*, and one with *-ity*. Then, make a set of 12 note cards with words that can take one of these suffixes, such as *danger*, *hesitate*, and *humid*.

- Ask a partner to work with the cards, placing them in the pockets of the suffixes they can use. Give your partner one point for each correct word combination.

- Repeat the process using your partner's cards.

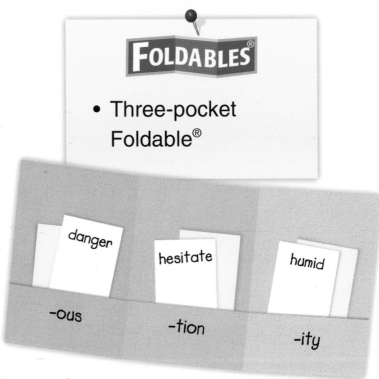

- Three-pocket Foldable®

Extension

- Pronounce, spell, and define each new word.

- Before space exploration there was travel on the high seas. Your task is to tell the story of "R Matey, the Pirate Who Stole the R," using such words as *stars, torch, arm, oar, are, yard, stare, rare, foghorn,* and other words with the sounds /är/, /âr/, and /ôr/.

- Write the title and the first paragraph of your adventure story, using as many /är/, /âr/, /ôr/ words as you can.

Extension

- Trade your story with a partner. Write the next paragraph of your partner's story with as many /är/, /âr/, /ôr/ words as you can. Trade back after three minutes.

- Write a conclusion to your story, and read it aloud to your partner, emphasizing the /är/, /âr/, /ôr/ sounds in the words.

Things you need:
- paper and pen or pencil
- dictionary

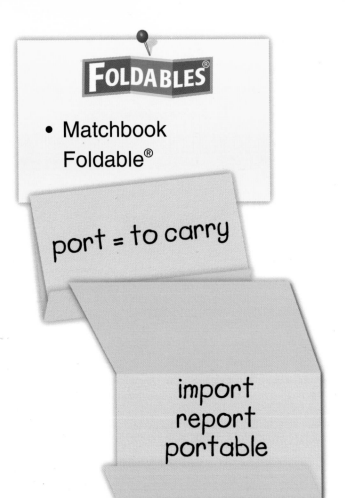

- Matchbook Foldable®

port = to carry

import
report
portable

- Use the dictionary to find root words from which you can build extensive word families.

- On the cover of a Matchbook Foldable®, write a root word and its definition. Inside the Foldable, write a list of "family words" (that is, words that contain the root word).

Extension

- Exchange Foldables with another student. Add words to his or her list.

- Use the dictionary to locate a variety of words that contain /ûr/ and /îr/ sounds. Some examples include *fur, word,* and *blur.* Try to find at least ten and write them in a list.

Extension

- With a partner combine your lists and write a rhyming poem, adding any other words you need for sense.

- Read the poem aloud together to another pair. See how many /ûr/ and /îr/ words each poem used.

Things you need:
- index cards
- pencils or markers
- dictionary

- On note cards write twenty words with unusual vowel sounds, such as *au* in *haul,* *aw* in *straw, ou* in *thought, au* in *daughter, ou* in *mountain, oy* in *loyal,* and *oi* in *boiling.*

- Work with a partner and use both decks.

- Turn over your cards one at a time. If both your card and your partner's card contain the same vowel sound, slap the cards and say, "Salsa!" If you slap the pile first, take it and put it aside. Nobody wins if the cards do not contain the same vowel sound.

Extension

- Use the cards to construct sentences, adding words as needed for sense.

Things you need:

- index cards
- dictionary
- pen or pencil

Latin and Greek Word Parts

- The prefix *bi-* stems from both Latin and Greek. It means "two." The suffix *-ism* comes from Latin and Greek as well. It refers to a belief, an act, or a condition.

- Write *bi-* on one pocket of a Two-pocket Foldable® and *-ism* on the other.

- Use a dictionary or go online to find three words that contain *bi-* and three that contain *-ism*. Write down the words and their definitions on note cards and place the cards in the correct pockets.

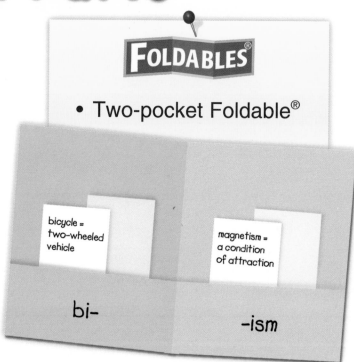

FOLDABLES®

- Two-pocket Foldable®

bicycle = two-wheeled vehicle

magnetism = a condition of attraction

bi–

–ism

Extension

- Write a paragraph that contains all the words in your Foldable.

Words with -ed and -ing

- Work with a partner. On a Three-Tab Foldable®, write "doubling -ed" on the first tab, "e drop, add -ed" on the second, and "no change, -ed" on the third.On your partner's Foldable, write the same directions, replacing -ed with *ing.*

- Switch Foldables with your partner. Underneath each tab, write a word that matches the directions for adding an inflectional ending.

Extension

- Write 20 verbs on cards. Place each card underneath the tab with the correct directions for adding -ed or -ing.

- Three-Tab Foldable®

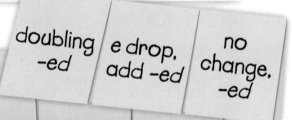

Greek and Latin Roots

• The Greek word part *astro-* means "star." The Latin word part *sci-* means "know." Use this information to write definitions for the words *astronomy, scientific, astrodome,* and *scientist.*

Extension

• Use a dictionary to check your definitions.

• Write a paragraph using each of these words and read it aloud to a partner.

Things you need:

• pen and paper
• dictionary

Phonics/ Word Study

- Write these VCCV words on note cards: *gallop, summon, vulture, valley, mustang,* and *absent.*

- Draw a line between the first and second syllable in each word.

- Using a Two-pocket Foldable®, sort the cards into two piles: Those that are divided between the same consonant should go in the left pocket, and those that are divided between different consonants should go in the right pocket.

Extension

- On a sheet of paper, write the plural form of each of your VCCV words.

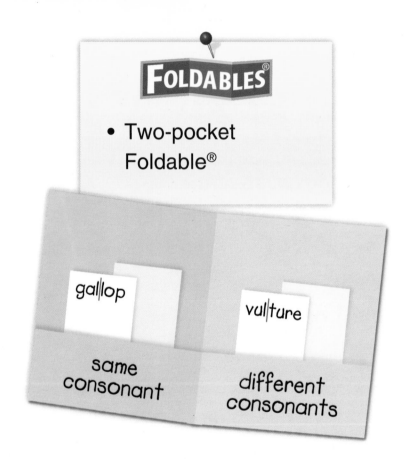

- Two-pocket Foldable®

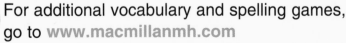

- Look in the dictionary for multiple-meaning words, such as *atmosphere*, *eye*, and *image*. Select and record ten words.

- For each word write two sentences. Each sentence should illustrate a different meaning of the word. For example, *Pollution is damaging Earth's atmosphere* and *The atmosphere at the party is joyous and festive.*

That girl has pretty eyes.

Thread the needle through the eye.

Extension

- Share your sentences with a partner. Using your sentences, have your partner state a definition for each multiple-meaning word.

Things you need:

- paper and pen or pencil
- dictionary

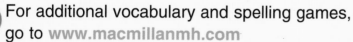

- In large letters write seven words with the V/V pattern on index cards, such as *poet* or *riot.*

- Divide the words into syllables by cutting the cards in half (or possibly thirds or fourths, depending on the number of vowels that the word contains). Shuffle the cards and arrange them in random rows. Have a partner reconnect the words. Award one point for each correct connection.

CRE ATE

Extension

- Arrange the words to try to form sentences, adding as few extra words as possible for sense.

- Read the sentences aloud to practice pronunciation.

Things you need:

- paper and pen or pencil

- index cards

- scissors

- dictionary

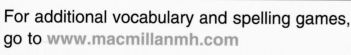
- Write a word on a note card and its homophone on the back of the card. Continue writing words until you have five pairs.

- Write one word from each pair on the pages of a Layered Book Foldable®.

- Switch Foldables with a partner. On each page of your partner's Foldable, write a homophone for each of your partner's words. The first of you to write all five homophones wins.

Extension

- Switch Foldables with another team and play the game again.

- Layered Book Foldable®

bridal bridle

- Look up three of your vocabulary words in a dictionary.

- Write a sentence for each vocabulary word on the tabs of a Three-Tab Foldable®. Use a comparison in each sentence as a context clue. For example, *The police car's* <u>*pursuit*</u> *was like a tiger going after its prey*.

Extension

- Give your sentences to a partner. Your partner should use your context clues to figure out the meaning of each word. Have your partner write these meanings underneath the tab of each sentence.

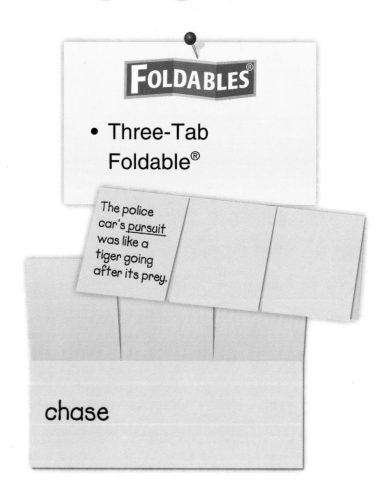

FOLDABLES®

- Three-Tab Foldable®

The police car's <u>pursuit</u> was like a tiger going after its prey.

chase

Consonant + *le*

- Make a list of 10 words that end in consonant + *le.* Include words with more than one syllable.

- Work with a partner. Pronounce the words aloud.

- Draw a line between each syllable. Discuss with your partner whether the syllables are open or closed.

Extension

- Choose four words from your list and write a paragraph using the words.

- Read your paragraph aloud to your partner.

jiggle

settle

Things you need:

- paper and pen or pencil

Word Parts: Affixes

- Working with a partner, make one set of cards with root words and a second set of cards with prefixes and suffixes. Write the root words in capital letters and the prefixes and suffixes in lowercase letters.

- Then, working together, see how many different words you can build from the cards. (Sometimes you may need to add a letter.) Write the words that you build on a sheet of paper.

Extension

- Have teams exchange cards and replay the game. Time the event.

- Use a dictionary to check your words. Allow one point for every word that is spelled correctly.

Things you need:

- index cards
- paper and pen or pencil
- dictionary

in   DESTRUCT   ible

Final /əl/ and /ən/

- Read a passage in a newspaper or magazine, and write on note cards all the words that end with an unaccented syllable where an *l* or an *n* follows a vowel. Say each word aloud.

- Using a Two-pocket Foldable®, mark the pockets with *l* and *n*. Place your cards in the correct pockets.

Extension

- Have a partner say the words aloud, and listen to make sure that the last syllable is unaccented.

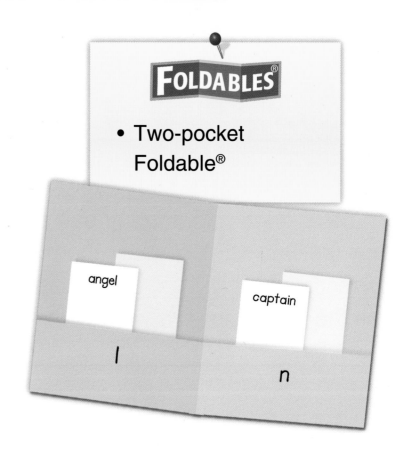

FOLDABLES®

- Two-pocket Foldable®

angel

captain

l

n

Homographs

- Using the dictionary make cards for five homographs, which are words that are spelled the same but are pronounced differently and have different meanings. Include the definition on each card. You should have a total of 10 cards.

- Then write a sentence for each word on a separate sheet of paper, leaving a blank for the homograph. Trade cards and sentences with a partner. Take turns completing each sentence aloud.

tear: liquid from the eye

tear: rip

Extension

- Play the game again with another pair. Whoever uses the most homographs correctly wins.

Things you need:
- index cards and paper
- pen or pencil
- dictionary

A _____ fell from his eye.

 Vocabulary PuzzleMaker

- Many English words are based on Greek and Latin roots. Some examples of Latin roots are *bi,* meaning "two", and *centum,* meaning "hundred". Some Greek roots include *tri,* meaning "three", and *bio,* meaning "life".

- Use a dictionary to find words built on each root.

Extension

- On the cover of a Matchbook Foldable®, write one of the word roots and its definition. Inside the Foldable, write the list of English words you found. Write how each word relates to the root.

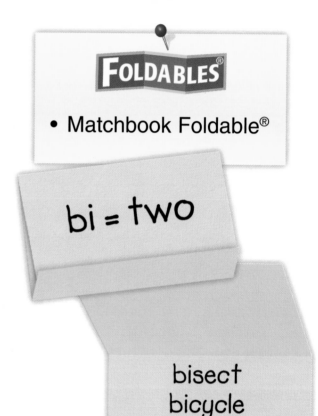

FOLDABLES®

- Matchbook Foldable®

bi = two

bisect
bicycle
biannual

Phonics/ Word Study

Multiple-Meaning Words

• With a partner scan the dictionary for multiple-meaning words. One of you can scan the entries for the letters A to M, and the other can scan the entries for the letters N to Z. Find one multiple-meaning word for each letter of the alphabet. Write the multiple meanings of each word.

Extension

• With a partner choose five of your words and write a sentence to illustrate the meaning of each word. Underline the words in the sentences.

Things you need:
• paper and pen or pencil
• dictionary

"Which cavity?"

- Using a Two-pocket Foldable®, mark one pocket with the suffix -*ance,* and the other with -*ence*.

- Then, make a set of 10 note cards with words that can take one of these suffixes, such as *differ* or *allow*.

- Ask a partner to work with the cards, placing them in the pockets of the suffixes they can use. Give your partner one point for each correct word combination. Repeat the process using your partner's cards.

Extension

- You and your partner can combine your cards and play again with another team.

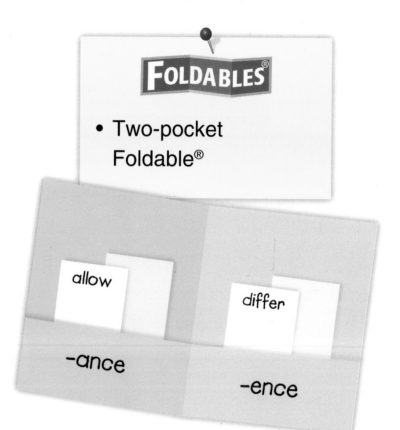

FOLDABLES®

- Two-pocket Foldable®

allow

differ

-ance

-ence

ANALOGIES: ANTONYMS

- Make 12 note cards with antonyms on each side. For example, if you write *safe* on one side of the card, write *dangerous* on the other side.

- Exchange cards with a partner. Looking at one side of each card, name an antonym for the word. Give one point for each correct antonym. If you or your partner gives a correct response that is not on the card, add the response to the card.

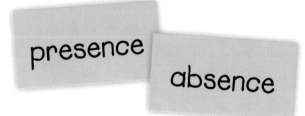

Extension

- Use the antonyms to make incomplete analogies on a sheet of paper. For example, write *presence : absence :: good : _____.* Create a list of ten analogies. Exchange lists with your partner and complete them.

Things you need:

- note cards
- pen or pencil
- dictionary and/or thesaurus

Homophones

- Write a pair of homophones on each door of a Four-Door Foldable®. Use two pairs of one-syllable words and two pairs of two-syllable words.

- Underneath each door, write a sentence for each word, but leave a blank where the homophone should be. Make sure to give context clues for the homophone.

- Trade Foldables with a partner. Fill in the blanks in their sentences with the correct homophones.

Extension

- Combine sentences with your partner, and play against another team.

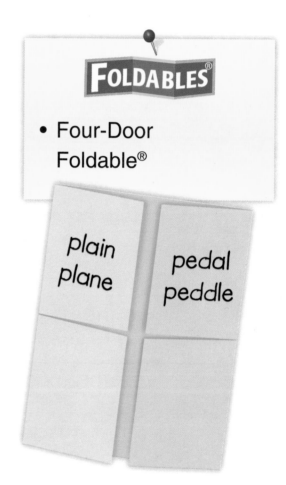

FOLDABLES®

- Four-Door Foldable®

plain plane

pedal peddle

Compound Words

- Write a list of eight compound words.

- Then write each part of each compound word on a separate card. Mix the cards up and turn them face down.

- Find a partner. Each player takes a card, looks at it, and takes another card. If they form a word, the player can keep the cards. If not, he or she replaces the cards, and the next player takes a turn. Whoever makes the most words wins.

Extension

- Combine your cards with those of another student pair and play with four sets of cards.

- Play as fast as you can by memorizing the words that are replaced on the table.

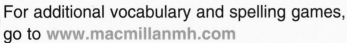

Things you need:

- paper and pen or pencil
- note cards
- dictionary

- Using a Two-pocket Foldable®, mark one pocket with the suffix *-less,* and the other with *-ness*.

- Then, make a set of 10 note cards with words that can take one of these suffixes, such as *kind* or *age*.

- Ask a partner to work with the cards, placing them in the pockets of the suffixes they can use. Give your partner one point for each correct word combination. Repeat the process using your partner's cards.

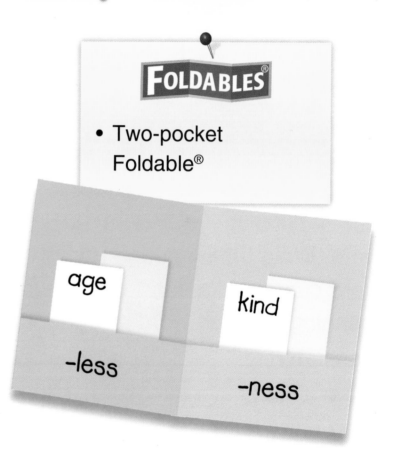

FOLDABLES®

- Two-pocket Foldable®

age

kind

-less

-ness

Extension

- You and your partner can combine your cards and play again with another team.

Greek Roots

- Many English words are based on Greek roots. Some examples of these Greek roots are *auto*, from the Greek word meaning "self, same"; *photo*, from the Greek word meaning "light"; and *tele*, from the Greek word meaning "far away."

- Use a dictionary to find words containing each of these Greek roots. Explain how each English word relates to its Greek root.

Extension

- On the cover of a Matchbook Foldable®, write one of the word roots and its definition. Inside the Foldable, write a list of English words that use the root.

- Matchbook Foldable®

auto = self

automobile
automatic
autobiography

Synonyms

- Write a list of six words having to do with contests of any kind, such as *regulations, outcome,* or *participants.*

- Using a thesaurus find one synonym for each word.

- With a partner write a newspaper article about a school contest, using as many of your words and synonyms as you can.

Extension

- Exchange articles with another pair of students.

- Circle all the synonyms you can find, using a different color or mark for each different set you locate.

Things you need:

- paper and pen or pencil

- markers

- thesaurus or dictionary

Words from Mythology

- Research the origins of the following words from mythology: *atlas, cereal, volcano, titan,* and *echo.*

- Write each word and a short description of its orign on the pages of a Layered Book Foldable®.

Extension

- Draw an illustration of each word on its Foldable page. Share it with a group.

- Post your Foldable pages on a word wall.

FOLDABLES®

- Layered Book Foldable®

atlas
cereal
volcano
titan
echo

Context Clues

- Make a list of six words from mythology with which your partner may be unfamiliar. Then write a sentence for each word using context clues to define the word.

- Trade sentences with a partner to see which words you can figure out.

Extension

- Combine your sentences with your partner's sentences. Challenge another team to define the words.

Things you need:
- paper and pen or pencil
- dictionary

- Label the doors of a Four-Door Foldable® with the number prefixes *uni-, bi-, tri-,* and *cent-,* so that each door has one prefix.

- Find two words in the dictionary that begin with each prefix. Write each word and its definition under the door of the prefix they contain. Review these words with a partner until both of you know them all.

Extension

- Create ten nonsense words with number prefixes. For instance, you could say that a "tritable" is a table with three sides. Quiz your partner about what each word might mean.

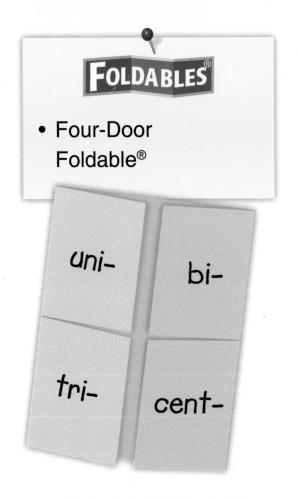

FOLDABLES®

- Four-Door Foldable®

 **Phonics/ Word Study**

Word Origins

- Use a dictionary to find the word origins of the following words: *reflected, tradition,* and *founding.*

- Make a table to chart the word, the language of origin, the word origin, and the meaning of that word origin.

Word	Language of Origin	Word Origin	Meaning

Extension

- Write the definition for each word you looked up. Tell how each word is related to the meaning of the word it comes from.

Things you need:
- paper and pencil
- dictionary

- Write words ending with *-able* or *-ible* on index cards, leaving out the *a* or the *i* in the suffix. On the back of each card, write the *a* or the *i* that correctly completes the word.

- With a partner use the cards as flash cards and practice spelling each other's words until both of you can spell all of the words correctly.

Extension

- Combine your words with your partner's, and repeat the activity with another team.

Things you need:
- index cards
- dictionary
- pen or pencil

a

i

vis ble

suit ble

poss ble

fashion ble

horr ble

- In the first column of a Foldable Chart®, list five Latin root words. In the second column, write the meaning of each Latin word. In the third column, write an English word that includes the Latin root.

- Cut the chart apart, mix up the pieces, and spread them out on your desk or table. Trade desks with a partner to rebuild the original chart.

Extension

- Take turns telling a story with your partner. Use a different Latin root word in each sentence you say. Try to use all the words.

FOLDABLES®

- Four-Door Foldable®

Words from Latin

scrib	to write	scribble